READING POWER

Extreme Machines

Dragsters

Scott P. Werther

The Rosen Publishing Group's

PowerKids Press™
New York

Published in 2002 by The Rosen Publishing Group, Inc.
29 East 21st Street, New York, NY 10010

First Edition

Book Design: Michelle Innes

Photo Credits: Cover, pp. 4, 5, 7, 8, 9, 10, 11 © Mike Campbell; pp. 12, 13 © Jon Ferrey; pp. 15, 17, 18, 19 © Mike Campbell; pp. 20, 21 © Chris Urso/AP Wide World Photos

Werther, Scott P.
Dragsters / Scott P. Werther.
   p. cm. – (Extreme machines)
Includes bibliographical references (p.   ) and index.
ISBN 0-8239-5953-8
1. Drag racing–Juvenile literature. 2. Dragsters–Juvenile literature. [1. Drag racing. 2. Automobiles, Racing.] I. Title.
GV1029.3 .W47 2001
796.72'0973–dc21

                                              00-013215

Manufactured in the United States of America

Contents

What Is a Dragster?   4

The Driver   14

The Crew   18

The Race   20

Glossary   22

Resources   23

Index   24

Word Count   24

Note   24

What Is a Dragster?

This car is a dragster.
It is a very long race car.

A dragster can go very fast.
It has a big engine.

7

A dragster has small wheels in the front. It has big wheels in the back.

9

A dragster has a big
wing at the back.
The wing helps the
car stay on the ground.

Dragsters have no brakes. They have parachutes to stop.

The Driver

The driver wears a helmet
and a thick suit.

The driver sits in the cockpit. There are bars to help the driver stay safe.

The Crew

The crew takes care of the car.
They check it before the race.

The Race

The race is over very quickly.
The red car has won.

Glossary

cockpit (**kahk**-piht) where the driver of a dragster sits

crew (**kroo**) the people who fix a car before and after a race

dragster (**drag**-ster) a special type of car made for racing

parachutes (**par**-uh-shoots) pieces of material that catch the air and slow down dragsters

Resources

Books
Drag Racing
by Jeff Savage
Silver Burdett Press (1998)

Dragsters: Cruisin'
by Maureen Connolly
Capstone Press (1992)

Web Sites:
Due to the changing nature of Internet links, PowerKids Press has developed an online list of Web sites related to the subject of this book. This site is updated regularly. Please use this link to access the list:
www.powerkidslinks.com/exmach/dragsters/

Index

C
cockpit, 16
crew, 18

D
dragster, 4, 6, 8,
    10, 12
driver, 14, 16

E
engine, 6

H
helmet, 14

P
parachutes, 12

S
suit, 14

W
wheels, 8
wing, 10

Word Count: 113

Note to Librarians, Teachers, and Parents

If reading is a challenge, Reading Power is a solution! Reading Power is perfect for readers who want high-interest subject matter at an accessible reading level. These fact-filled, photo-illustrated books are designed for readers who want straightforward vocabulary, engaging topics, and a manageable reading experience. With clear picture/text correspondence, leveled Reading Power books put the reader in charge. Now readers have the power to get the information they want and the skills they need in a user-friendly format.